For the Loneliness of Walking Out

Poems by

Sheila Black

LILY POETRY REVIEW BOOKS

Published by Lily Poetry Review Books
223 Winter Street
Whitman, MA 02382

https://lilypoetryreview.blog/

ISBN: 978-1-957755-47-2

For my friend Michele Marcoux
whose paintings continue to inspire my poems

Table of Contents

*"Reading what I have just written, I now believe
I stopped precipitously, so that my story seems to have been
slightly distorted, ending, as it did..."*

Louise Glück, "Afterword"

Small Green Island

We went to the abandoned mansions
and studied what was left in them—a strand
of fake pearls in a puddle of stained
water, a few plastic milk jugs, condoms
which we steered away from, needles
the same, dolls—parts of doll bodies,
the plastic often cracked—some strange
bloodless version of what harm might
come. We felt safe because we knew
how to climb trees, how to place ourselves
in the crown—a world of green heights.
And the smell of rain. We knew how to
dip our fingers in hibiscus, bougainvillea.
We knew the sadness of the colonists
in the gardens left to rot, in the oddities
placed on the beach, parts of ships
denuded by salt and storm until they
resembled broken lives. We knew to
put our ears to shells. We knew what
they gave back was not actually ocean
but the noise of our own blood.

Elegy for Avenue B

Even the trees had jaundice
that winter, waistlines thinned to
needles. Eyes, strings that disintegrated.
Love, sex, death. Anecdotes of
how fast they went. And the sweet
guile of the approach, a gleaming wood
surface, razored, marked with
rings that interlocked. Bourbon, beer,
the sharp edge of a lime. I kicked
the leaves to the curbs, eyed the backs
of strangers. My fury had been
for nothing. I saw that now. Life
was colder, blood-gleam of spilled
pennies by a door, grit trail of
cigarettes, bottle caps we made into
trees along Tompkins Street Bar.
The owner and his sons would be
dead by March. It happened that way.
Out with a cold one week, in Saint
Vincent's the next. And love the
incarnadine. A whoosh of gasoline
on asphalt streets, horse races on
the television screen above the bar,
when the black mare broke her leg,
we lost our bet and stumbled out
to a milky oblivion of stars.

Lontaine

1.

For a long time I had struggled toward such clarity,

the mouth of ash & not the film,

in which I was free to
flicker and enter as I chose. To give in too easily to "wanting

the impossible," now seemed

a repudiation of the skin as it breathes, the facticity of another's

breath, tasting of onions or cigarettes,
thin wine or yeasted bread, a decay to be

embraced & to hesitate a betrayal of the truer forms:

the scudding clouds or the sunlight which strips

bare, much as winter does.

2.

In those days, I often walked

without direction, not infrequently seized by
a longing to fling myself

down to the earth, to dig a hole & pour my voice in.

Afraid, at times, I might start hugging the trees—

blood sister of cherry, moon-bark of aspen,

Often, I wondered at my purpose—

this dogged sorrow, which had taught me so little,

until I understood I was struggling to construct myself around
an absence:

what-I-desired-and-could-not-will-to-be.

3.

When autumn came, the pain attenuated to almost-pleasure:

the world now limpid, my mirror—

pale grass, high wind, bruise clouds drifting over,

even the somehow tortured-looking shapes of the junipers.

Ice filled the space behind my eyes. I believed I had never

seen each object in the world so clearly

or understood what desert and plain and forest might mean,

those spaces where people still enter

as alien, outside the range of hearth or village, town or strip-mall,

far from creature comfort.

4.

Rain pelted and turned to hail.

Icicles coalesced along the edges of the buildings.

One morning the car refused to start.

I walked until my fingers were blue, and I was afraid to look at my toes,
like ice-fish, deep under a lake, the fact that they freeze

in place, sometimes years.

5.

You left on a journey and came back

tanned and speaking loudly. I pretended not to notice
the precise manner of you not noticing me,

winter inside, a hunger for eternity,

until I believed I understood even the trees gloved in ice,
the meekness of lawns, the grasses' inexorable stiffening,

believed I would stay awake through any operation,

which was why I watched you, just watched you,
regardless of the pain it caused me,

or my refusal of all consolation,

so long had I sought to enter the realm of pure feeling.

The Home Front, 1992

The way you held your wrists
as if expecting some heavy gift—
a basket of bread that sounds
hollow when you tap on it, golden
and feathered on the tongue, a split plum
too juicy for the thin skin to hold it in,
frozen grapes with their silvered
glow. We lay there, and you told a story
about a desert you walked, something
terrible happened that you wouldn't
name but lingered like a pall in the air,
a stone held under your tongue.
You tasted its salt. Once you
said "I didn't know anyone who
died." I thought you were telling
me you were lucky, but all you
were saying was you didn't know
anyone you'd killed. Mornings,
you turned your back to me, cupping
your coffee. You liked to look at trains,
you liked to watch the blackbirds rise
from the onion fields at the edge of town,
half in love with how they hold
themselves together yet so apart.
I could already see the time I wouldn't
know you anymore, when I'd mistake
your back for the back of a different man.
Once you said you found a dead horse
out there; someone had wrapped a scarf
of blue silk around its neck; that was love.
You knew it, and you sat there alone
a long time until they came to drag you
to base. I could already see when all this
would be gone—a memory like a coin

at the bottom of a fountain covered
in moss. I knew what I would keep—
an image of red birds in heavy snow,
pecking the ground for a seed that skitters
just out of reach. Down by the river
a person flapping their arms in blue light.

Amaryllidaceae

1.

In my dream state of New Mexico, the onion
fields sing and breathe. They know

how to discard a skin without regret,
but also, how to make beauty

of what is lost. In this dream state,
I hand you armfuls of onions that desiccate

in the clear clear desert air. They resemble
the wings of moths

or translucent birds. They fly through the hot
wind.

They land at our feet.

2.

I never told you I loved you.

I find it amusing in a bitter-almond way,
the elaborate prohibitions I set

around these words that still carve

a hole in me, bone-smooth, bone-dry,

filled with wings of onions.

3.

Our dream state was border uncomfortable.

Sometimes I was your stalker.
Sometimes you almost needed me.

I misinterpreted every word you said.
Or fretful, transcribed, revised.

This was the madness

that Sophocles found age redeemed him from.

What is the inscription for loving what doesn't
love you back?

4.

Lessons of distance. Lessons of time versus space.
Lessons of relative weight.

I am planting onions. Their flowers resemble
lilium, resemble daffodils,

resemble narcissi stripped back to
pure form,

as Narcissus himself was stripped.
What could be more horrible than to find

you love only yourself?

The bulb in the ground, the bloom which is
somewhat flavorless,

but nevertheless edible.

5.

In my dream state of New Mexico, I cover
myself with onion flowers.

I know the truth is the hollow my body makes in this red earth.

On this bare red hill where I never

told you what I was most possessed
to say.

6.

Now the November fields,
rust of the used world.

Do you remember how the tall grasses bleach as they die?

Nothing else resembles that bleach-shine, not gold,
but the ghost of what gold is; the ghost skins,

rising. We want most to love

what actually happened.

Linnets

But still a hole in the air
when I walk the road with the high cheat grass
sprigs on either side, and the shrike, the wire bird,

the one with the curved beak and quiet song, known
to impale field mice along the spikes. We love at times
what is vicious, then that viciousness haunts us

so we turn in our sweaty sheets, review, rewind
the empty night as if something we were presenting
to someone, opening our palms to show its pure shine.

The linnet is known for its flight call—an ascent so
stirring the linnet is a prized cage bird in many places,
locked in so its notes can be heard at will, the

charge they deliver to the silver air.

Medea Rising

I recognize only her wild hair,
which circles round her face like a blue fire,

her face a mask of eye-holes
        and mouth-holes

from which a sinister iris opens with its blue
        and yellow tongue.

        She says, "Don't look at that,"

and she is wearing a raincoat, holding two grocery bags,

        sacks loaded with eggs, potatoes, pork chops,
a violent purple eggplant.

        She waves her hand, riding a bus through rain,
through the outskirts. She presses her face to the glass

        whose pattern of droplets resembles a tenderness. She is holding
something green between her fingers,

a kind of nascent web like the ghost
        grass of spring.

        She wants me to know this is how it begins—a growing
like kudzu over the ordinary garages,

        the mailboxes. She shows me a box which opens in her chest;
inside a fledgling, already fierce and wild,

        some kind of goshawk or marsh hawk with gold dopplering
the edges of its fluffy wings.

        She wants me to know this was what she saw: an egg
of fire with a winged heart inside it.

Rembrandt, 1639

Tell them of the sheen of indigo—
how it spears at the edge

of certain summer skies, noon
when shadows shrink, the sky

swallows its mouthful of black.

I see the irises on her table,
the sharp lemon

of their insides. I can spare her
nothing. They will all die

before me. I don't know this yet,
only the men coming

to count the canvases,
which I call "my children,"

though they are hardly alive.
What waits for me: bruise

nights on streets where rain falls
in a steady stream. My wooden

shoes will split. I used to think
I might float if I walked

quickly enough. I have grown
much too heavy, I think.

To paint shadow you must use all
the colors—crimson lake,

flake white, layering until as when
you wet two fingers,

a candle flame gutters out—traces
all that remain.

I have squinted into skies
until trees and houses melt.

Did I ever do more than merely
imitate? Tell them of the sheen—

its color terrible and mute
like God. Over my head, starlings,

sparrows circle through lowering
clouds. The house is packed,

the wagons filled. A bailiff fastens
the last window shutter, then

the oaken door.

Elegy with Orion

I don't believe in the stars exactly or the man
who told me my palm was cut in two
by "love troubles," but I spot Orion every time I
tilt my head to look up this time of year—
days shortening, the promise of pure winter.
Brother, hunter, rapist, victim of something like a lynching,
murdered by Artemis for his unspeakable crimes.
There he is eternally chasing the stag,
eternally glimmering with his quiver.
Here are the stars tonight, such cunning fairy lights,
close up no more than maws of fire, swallowing
whatever would breathe beside them.
I have loved you best in glimmers.
I don't know what I would do with you if I had you,
closer than a tangent veering off into deepest
space; yet still shadowing as Orion shadows me,
a kind of *imago*, which spells out the ancient grief
of how bad a person can be and still be
beloved. The Greeks were smarter
than we are about such things; they knew
longing makes you cruel, knew
what you love best can destroy you. I remember
one night with you in a bar, the stories we
traded—childhood favorites—*The Snow Queen*.
Her splinter enters the boy's eye, and the girl
travels to find him; only her tears will make
the world beautiful again. I loved that story once,
but now I think it as troubling as the hunter,
the good brother, terrible guest, who pillages
where he can. See how even now
he struggles to find a way home.

Amaryllis

I'm thinking why, why
do you pick yourself up?
The long leaf split down the middle,
browning and ugly,
what is left of copal,
sepal, *seed*. But yours
remains swollen no matter
what. I have pushed you into
my mudroom, my hall closet
of rubber boots. Left
you on my splintered deck
through ice and a rain so hard
one might swear the air itself was
converting. I have spilled your
earth, picked at your two leaves
with nervous fingers, left my own
holes, my newly crafted scars
all over your greenish body. Yet
each year, right around this time,
I watch you begin again. What
will it help if I tell you how your
blossoms break me—so red
and wide and filled with gold.

Medea Talks About the Weather

(1)

The sun comes out and the soul misses
the storm clouds,

all day gathering, hovering as if a ceiling
was about to break,

the sky split like a finger sliced by glass,
a sluicing, some thing

born. Instead, the normal cottonwoods
with their sinister water smell,

and why sinister when in a desert
find the cottonwoods and you find

the water you need to fill your humble tin
cup, but who doesn't secretly love

the storm, the idea that even the roof
over your head might be lifted and swirled?

(2)

She tells me this was her sin, her grief.
She wanted it all to burn, but after

the ashes on her eyelashes and tongue—no,
even the palms of her hands,

the simple objects of day telling her
she was dust—or worse.

The worm mouth ever open,
digesting the world,

reducing it to pulp.

(3)

Was this necessary?
She wonders at her own story, fingers

its threads as she rides the late bus across
town. She is old, a sack of brittle

bone inside a furred red cloak that is torn now,
like a mouth that has dared to speak

whatever it wished once too often. She can't
remember his face or his slate-colored eyes

turning her to lava, a finger breaking the sky
into two parts that will not meet—

silver and rain, the promise
of a love that would end time.

Dawn Chorus

Those years the bed felt like a boat,
and our limbs were always pressed against
the limbs of sick children, the hair in the mouth,
the stumbling—floral, immense—down the hall
for the sticky, sickly, cherry-flavored medicine.
One coughed, then another; one turned
into a dream which made them moan in terror.
And the awake dry-mouthed mother who
believes/has learned the dream is merely life.
But what joy in that wide bed, the birds in their
dawn chorus, the trickster ones who sang
in the middle of the night as if to say moon
was sun, time was not or would not ever be
as it had been. An owl coughs from a tree.
A child coughs back. Later we would think
we had thought this forever—our bodies tied
to them as if by thin moonlight threads,
but it was only a season, a rotation. The
swallows' nests left behind each year to
crumble into dust, littering the back porch
with their intricate broken weaving.

Your Spirit Will Need to Rest After it is Cleaned

The skunk has taken residence under
the house—sprays often, when the dog barks,
when we run the vacuum cleaner, when
the footsteps of our quarantine pass overhead.
So much frightens it. I spotted it this morning
lumbering along the driveway. Pregnant.
The skunk is pregnant, which makes me reconsider
my previous plan—to locate someone
willing to brave the virus and remove
this skunk from its bower below my kitchen
sink. What changes? Four months in lockdown,
I pass time like Alice-down-the-rabbit-hole,
rapt before my many ethereal screens,
which fill now with postcard-sized faces.
I turn off my devices. I sit out on the deck
under flowering wisteria, branches twisting
sensuously in a high wind that may turn
to tornado. Let the skunk be safe. Let me live
with its animal smell in my nostrils—familiar
signal of fear, longing. Let me hold in my hand
a few grains of soil, pat them around the base
of this wisteria here, which springs from a hole
someone sawed in the deck—almost too tight
to breathe, but it does. I can smell its colors—
violet-damp, petals, dew, the warmth
of sun they hold. Let me praise the miracle—
how far the light must travel to be turned
inside them into this bright sap they share.

Descanso

Go lightly. The way pain enters each day.

Light the candle of flowers that blooms
half-desiccated on the roadside.

South Texas, south San Anto.

The truck was parked through the hot morning.

No one heard the cries that rose from it.
Or recognized them as cries.

The purveyor on his cell phone in a field.

The white-yellow-red-black-speckled birds
that flew into the sky at the same time.

A bare branch as a form of punctuation.

When the hospitals flung open their doors and emergency bays
it was too late. They only waited over the blinking

coffee machines. No one felt a single breath of cold
but everyone wished to.

Go sweetly, the way pain

enters. Or stop and put out a vase of flowers
for them, understanding in some appalled intimate way

how close they were.

Mother/Medea

I trained my children to be anti-capitalist
and now I work to support them.

The worm in the apple—does it have to be a worm?

I am trying to love my bones' brittle, to love
the mind without the inevitable trap door,

what for so long I poured into lust or longing,
now phantom-ache, pines in snow.

My children don't like me enough.
My husband gaslights out of habit or lack of imagination.

I am drawing a door with ice-blue chalk on the beige wall
of the second bedroom.

I am practicing the chords for "Everybody Hurts,"
planting sunflowers so they grow fence-high.

To erase the difficult self. To take a name and refigure
it into another's—

Medea is the trap door in this poem. She burns with gorgeous
indigo. Terror is the needle of her spine.

"Here is the worst you can do," she says, her rage
like a green-black wave, higher than my head

as she teaches me clenched finger at a time
to dive down.

Medea Among the Spiders

The orb weavers have returned,
each one almost

the size of a palm—each shaped
like the belly

of a mother, backs rainbowing
under the thick rain

that falls and falls. *You poor thing,*
she says, *Wake up.*

Silver threads in her hair, silver
threads stretched across

the walkway—here, between the plumeria,
between the sad extravagance

of bougainvillea, the superb bird of paradise.
What else did you think garden meant?

The chord from your own belly,
cinnamon, blood—in your memory

root from which they flowered,
root from which they ran

and spread—and to love them so,
like the orb weavers reaching

with their eight arms
to grasp a thread so thin it disappears.

The Earth

What can I tell her over breakfast when she says
her son suffers from madness, and because there
is no mental health, he has ended up in jail,
and she is relieved, because at least he might
be safe there or he might get to see the doctor.
We are eating egg white omelets; we are counting
carbs; we are buttoning ourselves in our clean dresses
and high-heeled shoes in order to bring home the bacon,
doing what we need to do, and "It is what it is."
Her granddaughter and daughter are living with her
in the one bedroom. Nights, the daughter lounges by
the pool, looking at her phone, while she teaches the child
to plant seeds in a flower bed she feels bad she does not own.
She tells me she cried in the car coming here; she did not know
me then. She thought we would be talking to each other
the whole time about what we are selling, what
the other might buy, but somehow we left that behind
over the toast with the cunning little pots of strawberry jam.
Who can explain all this luxury, all this despair?
Or how we all hold our secret shames so close
and gloss our lips with "Cinnamon Fire" as if that were
some legitimate form of protection. Cinnamon Fire!
She just turned fifty. I tell her wait ten years—you
won't know more, but you will get closer to forgiving,
because it is all happening on a wheel that spins
so fast. Why not stop and look at the pink flowers
you've planted with your granddaughter? Why not dig
your bare toes in the good wet earth? We play with the crusts
on our plates. The waitress takes the coffee away. We
are strangers again, each carrying our lonely fear
our children won't find their way, wishing for them
some inner logic—sacred trust of self and earth, which exists
for each of us so far within, so far under the skin, we can't

even begin to say what it is made of. It merely is,
poised between love and grief, the blue space we call wonder
which is merely the dew on the grass, shadow the sun
makes as it rolls over the vast skin of the Earth.

Dear Reader

Chekhov, of course, someone brave
and good. He sets out, coughs into a large
handkerchief, the kind we know from
our grandmothers. A roseate of blood
or two, a quicker pulse. He boards the wagons,
the trains, the donkey backs that will
carry him some 6,000 miles to Sakhalin.
Here, even young boys learn
snow must be folded to form walls.
The prisoners deface park benches, rest
in their own filth, *sorry* taking root
until a person merely repeats its catechisms,
though this only makes them more
miserable. Have you never been there?
Wanting to scrape your name in
the dirt, rend whatever is put in your hands?
Easy to misread—though Chekhov did not,
understanding for every scrawled *no*, deeper
inside a bird of fire flickers with ghost-desire:
to drink in every morning as if it were new.
On the way home, he carries 10,000 testimonies,
a slight sick vertigo as he writes of lives
iced-over—the ones who sink into their beds
each night with only a hunger to
cradle. Dear Reader, it is a skill to hold
oneself apart, to report only what is and not
what one might will or hope. Chekhov who writes
"Don't tell me the moon is shining."

Everywhere and Nowhere at the Same Time

It is a race against the sun. I think of you as I
pace the hot yard, trying to resurrect the pepper
plant, begging it with my artificial rain to unfurl
its yellowing leaves. It is a race against the moon—
that moment of stepping into dark as into
ocean, believing for the span of a few breaths
there is no boundary here. Your face floats in stars,
emerges from an indeterminate mass of
cloud. This is what it is to be ghosted. I know
what comes back is my own echo; yet how can it not
be blended in some way with what you were? I
am watching two leaves emerge from the dry earth,
a tiny fleck of green, and how it divides, divides.
Every day, acute miracles of becoming. Each day,
the shadows folding up their umbrellas to walk home.

Medea Talks About Our Stars

I tell her, "Listen, I was always timid."
"Not timid," she says, "ashamed."

I look at her in her ragged red dress,
her bare feet and cracked toes,

her eyes so ravenous I look away,
but even when I brush past,

even when I mutter, "You don't understand,"
she clings to me like the smoke

of a charred meat—goat maybe, roasted
in a pit with branches of oregano

burning their green into the blackened bits of wood
left on the ground.

"Watch my lips," she says,
"No safety,"

and I think of how in the night I have hugged myself,
so lonely I felt like a blade of the moon,

some sort of chipped metal, a mezzaluna
over a board of onion

skins and tears. All she would like me to do
is sit down with her at a table

and drink stewed tea in the bleached morning.
All she cares about is that I acknowledge

the brutal stars of love—the ways we are nothing
without their serrated daggers, breathing as we do

so briefly under their long dead lights.

Deep Sea

The numbers have departed from my father
but he can still tell a story

of how he once commandeered a gifted drunken
pilot from Tallahassee to San Diego

by helicopter. They flew in the early mornings
over corn and soybean fields,

sometimes rolled a time down the highways
with the tractors and work trucks

or hovered low to land at gas stations and motels,
juke joints and blues joints.

My father's hands now resemble the deep sea paper
skins of fishes we have never seen;

he waves them in front of his cataracted eyes
as though they might disintegrate at any moment.

Math has deserted him. When asked to count backwards
from 100, he roams further afield

than one might imagine, swooping through the 10,000s
as though exploring a depthless ocean.

We used to believe there was nothing down there, but
the force of life is its ability to give off its own light—

even when there is none. Look how violent stars
burn in the blank of space and through us.

My father wants me to feel the oily heat of those roads
stuck in the past, the faded red Fords or Dodges,

the men working the fields, who had so little they
could hold it in their two hands.

The pilot struggled with solitary desperations—an antic
humor in a crowd followed by the nightly ritual

of holding a loaded gun to his head. My father's
job to talk him down. My father said he felt like

a swimmer through indigo waters. He was twenty-two.
He knew nothing and so he pretended,

which seemed, at the time, almost enough. The pilot
found ten years later in a motel in Encino.

My father says, "You don't need to hear that part."
He shows me a snapshot, wildly discolored,

their blue dragonfly-shaped copter about to touch down
on a road lined with live oaks; in the background a farm stand,

someone selling summer tomatoes and peaches. A swirling
motion in the air as if all you would need to do

to go there was touch it. What is it to breathe light into
the darkest spaces of the world? Down where

voices mean nothing, where it always night
and snowing.

We Shall Rest

The elm split by lightning stands
above the bench where my father sat
the summer he could no longer breathe
enough to walk to the Avalon
without stopping. I sat next to him,
a little bored, a little tired of
his childlike need—his insistence
on walking even when he could not
walk. In the film we watched
that day, a group of actors are
rehearsing a play. The star runs through
his lines in the car in which he is
driven to and fro from his hotel
to the provincial but charming theater.
He is a person who cannot express
what he feels. But as he runs his lines
with his driver, a young sullen girl, who
appears disinterested but is not, we see
they are telling each other everything
through the borrowed words—speaking
of an estate, an orchard, some cherry
trees. My father fell asleep, woke
startled, querulous. He'd enjoyed what
he'd seen and wanted to see it again,
so we stayed, mouthing the lines of
Uncle Vanya along with the actors on screen,
though we never discussed the film after.
Half the elm is dead—gray branches,
a seam along the trunk, but the other half
appears to flourish, fanning outward,
the fresh, green, tear-shaped leaves.
I can no longer even be annoyed by
my father, which feels like the very
definition of being mortal. The trunk of

the elm tilts slightly to catch the light from
the shadows of buildings on either side.
With luck it will live 300 years.

We Keep Living

You return to Beirut, the edge of the war,
to hold your ninety-one-year-old mother's
hand in the hospital where you
were born, after your family was forced
out of Jerusalem. Meanwhile, I make
lists for the grocery, try to sell spots
in classes. I tell someone that telling their
story will help them uncover their soul.
I am ashamed after at what that word
soul might mean. No rain for a hundred
days, and then the late monsoons, the
palms whipping back and forth as if
in ecstasy. I write you *everyone is fine*,
then cross out what I have written and
start again. There is no word for what
happens in the rooms of death—that abrupt
clouding behind the eyes. Or for how
in one place a person contemplates boiled
chicken with maybe some spring asparagus,
while in another a whole city is flattened,
and the world rolls on. I try to grasp
the voices of the ones who keep calling
for what they term "a difficult necessity,"
by which they mean the right to commit
atrocity. It rains all night, and the streets
gleam. You write me an email about the work
you do: building hospitals, strange to walk
through this one, where you were born and
your mother is dying, both exiled, at the edge
of a war that only flares down intermittently.

I drink a cup of tea, chop onions in twilight.
I remember you holding wide your arms for
your child, who ran towards you, head tilted
down, with the speed of a bullet train.

For the Loneliness of Walking Out

So often it is a garden where you learn
grief. The person leaves,

but the colors of the petals do not change.
A brightness

punctuated by insect wings, the whir
of life now unfolding, now

turning in, as I folded you inside me
like a garden behind a high wall,

green and inimical to me and what I
might become. Mouth of dust which made

me picture the flat snake mouth, the flat
tongue slithering out into the world.

A picture—snow globe perfect:
the webbing of tree branches, a place where I

for a time forgot where my skin ended,
the world began.

Letter in Spring

Needless to say, I am still plumping
for the orange tree to come back,
even though its thin dead twigs, frozen
in our unexpected polar vortex freeze,
seem to promise otherwise. I'm still
convinced I will run into you
along the Riverwalk or under the oaks,
and we will be able to pick up
the thread as if it never broke. I'm still
holding out hope that my husband's
cloud of pessimism will abruptly lift,
and he will bring me lilies, armfuls of them,
for the Easter that never was in which
we all rise up as out of our graves to live
doubly so. I'm telling you—him—come out
here. Look at the train tracks and the
tender shape of the yellow dog who has
lived here wild, but begging when she
needs to, longer than us even. Look at
the cardinals, the pair of them, how they
scoot a little impatiently from branch
to wire fence and back. Do you think
they are arguing over whether to stay—
why this yard and not the one next door?
Do you think, like us, they have learned
to love our mutilated mountain laurel,
half-dead bougainvillea, this mighty
orange tree, now a ghost, which year
after year managed, despite its diminutive
size, to yield so many, such oranges?
My husband has his eyes to the binoculars.

He is telling me he heard owls again
last night. Sometimes we feel as distant
as continents but really we are like the
ocean beneath, full of large animals sending
signals across cold blue waters.

Notes:

"Descanso." (p.21) On June 27, 2022, 53 people were found dead in and around a tractor-trailer near Lackland Air Force Base in San Antonio, Texas. The deaths, caused by heat exposure and asphyxiation, occurred during an effort to smuggle migrants across the U.S.-Mexico border in a time of increased border militarization.

"Dear Reader," (p.52) references Anton Chekhov's trip to the island of Sakhalin in the summer and autumn of 1890, during which he took some 10,000 testimonials from prisoners on the island. The book he wrote *Sakhalin Island* consists of his travel notes and investigation of prison conditions.

Acknowledgments

Grateful acknowledgment is made to the following publications in which these poems first appeared:

The Black Fork Review, "Small Green Island"
Newfound, "Elegy for Avenue B"
Jet Fuel Review, "Lontaine"
The Baltimore Review, "The Home Front, 1992"
Third Point Press, "Amaryllidaceae"
Red Coyote, "Linnets"
Quiet Lightning, "Medea Rising," "Medea Talks About the Weather," and "Medea Talks About our Stars"
Talking Writing, "Rembrandt, 1639"
Press 54, "Elegy with Orion"
300 Days of Sun, "Amaryllis"
Cumberland River Review, "Dawn Chorus"
Connecticut River Review, "Your Spirit Will Need to Rest After it is Cleaned"
Stonecoast Review, "Descanso"
Blackbox Manifold, "Mother/Medea," and "Everywhere and Nowhere at the Same Time"
Rock & Sling, "Medea Among the Spiders"
Poem-a-Day, Academy of American Poets, "The Earth"
Thuya Review, "Dear Reader"
Lily Poetry Review, "Deep Sea" and "Letter in Spring"
Zocalo Public Square, "We Shall Rest"
Southern Florida Poetry Journal, "We Keep Living"
The Stillwater Review, "For the Loneliness of Walking Out"

Much of this book was written at a residency at the Hosking Houses Trust, 33 Duck Lane, The Square, Stratford-upon-Avon, Warwickshire CV37, UK. I want to profoundly thank Sarah Hosking for her warmth, friendship, and her support of women writers and artists over forty.

About the Author

Sheila Black is the author of five poetry collections and three chapbooks. Her most recent collection is *Radium Dream* (Salmon Poetry Ireland, 2022). She is a co-editor of *Beauty is a Verb: The New Poetry of Disability* (Cinco Puntos Press, 2011), named a Notable Book for Adults for 2012 by the American Library Association. She is a 2012 Witter Bynner Fellow with the Library of Congress, for which she was selected by Philip Levine. Poems and essays have appeared in *Blackbird, The Birmingham Review, Kenyon Review Online, Poetry, The Nation, The New York Times,* and elsewhere. She lives in San Antonio, TX and Tempe, AZ where she is assistant director of the Virginia G. Piper Center for Creative Writing at Arizona State University (ASU).

www.ingramcontent.com/pod-product-compliance
Lightning Source LLC
Chambersburg PA
CBHW030526130626
46549CB00007B/3119